God's Grandeur

Dawn Hallier

God's Grandeur

First published 2021 by Beaten Track Publishing

Print ISBN: 978 1 78645 522 2
eBook ISBN: 978 1 78645 523 9

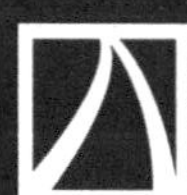

Beaten Track Publishing,
Burscough, Lancashire.
www.beatentrackpublishing.com

My grateful thanks to my publisher Debbie, who has been a pleasure to deal with throughout the making of this book.
Her suggestions have been immensely helpful and nothing has been too much trouble. I have enjoyed every moment of the process.

For my daughters, Glynnis and Colleen;

My grandchildren, Richard and Jessica;

My great-grandchildren, Killian, Cadence and Abigail.

Also for Grant and Lauren, Mike and Amy.

With love and gratitude.

To dear Craig and Erica, with my love.

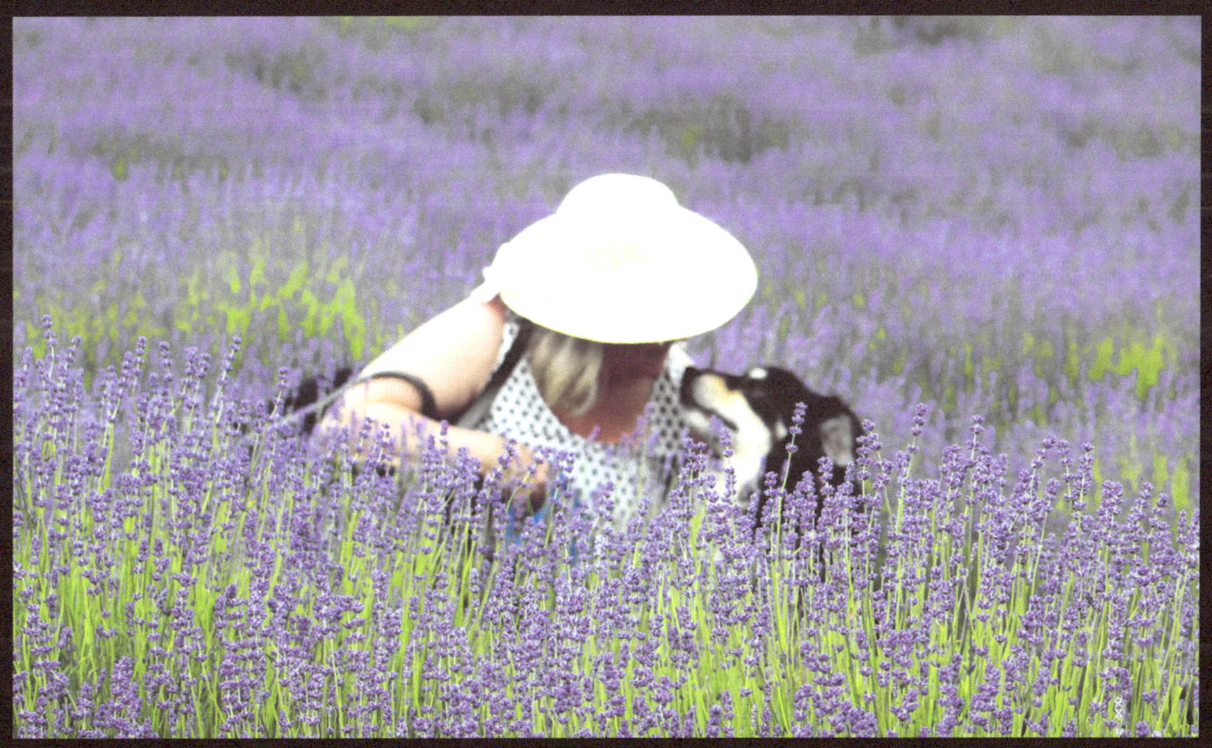

The prose in this book was mostly written in England between 1993 and 1995 with only a few pieces written in the past year or so.

The great beauty of England was, and remains, a constant source of joy and delight. The warmth, courtesy and gentleness of the British people has also been an inspiration. These are beautiful and enduring qualities which are ever worthy of celebration. We should always be aware of such qualities, especially in an age where it sometimes becomes increasingly difficult to see them, and where it becomes ever more important to remember that they do indeed exist.

We should greatly value these good and true aspects of our nature and continue to inculcate them into a younger generation so as not to leave a barren space in their hearts and minds.

It is my wish that the prose and photographs in this book will help us all in that endeavour.

Now it is dusk and the snow lies deep upon the ground. The village and surrounding fields, all now are wrapped in mystery. Snowflakes swirl and dance through the air before drifting to lie pure and unblemished in the lanes. Street lamps cast pools of soft radiance and tall trees throw deep shadows on glistening snow. All is deeply peaceful and still. From cottage windows, lamps glow warm and welcoming and seem to speak of all that is harmonious, of all that is good.

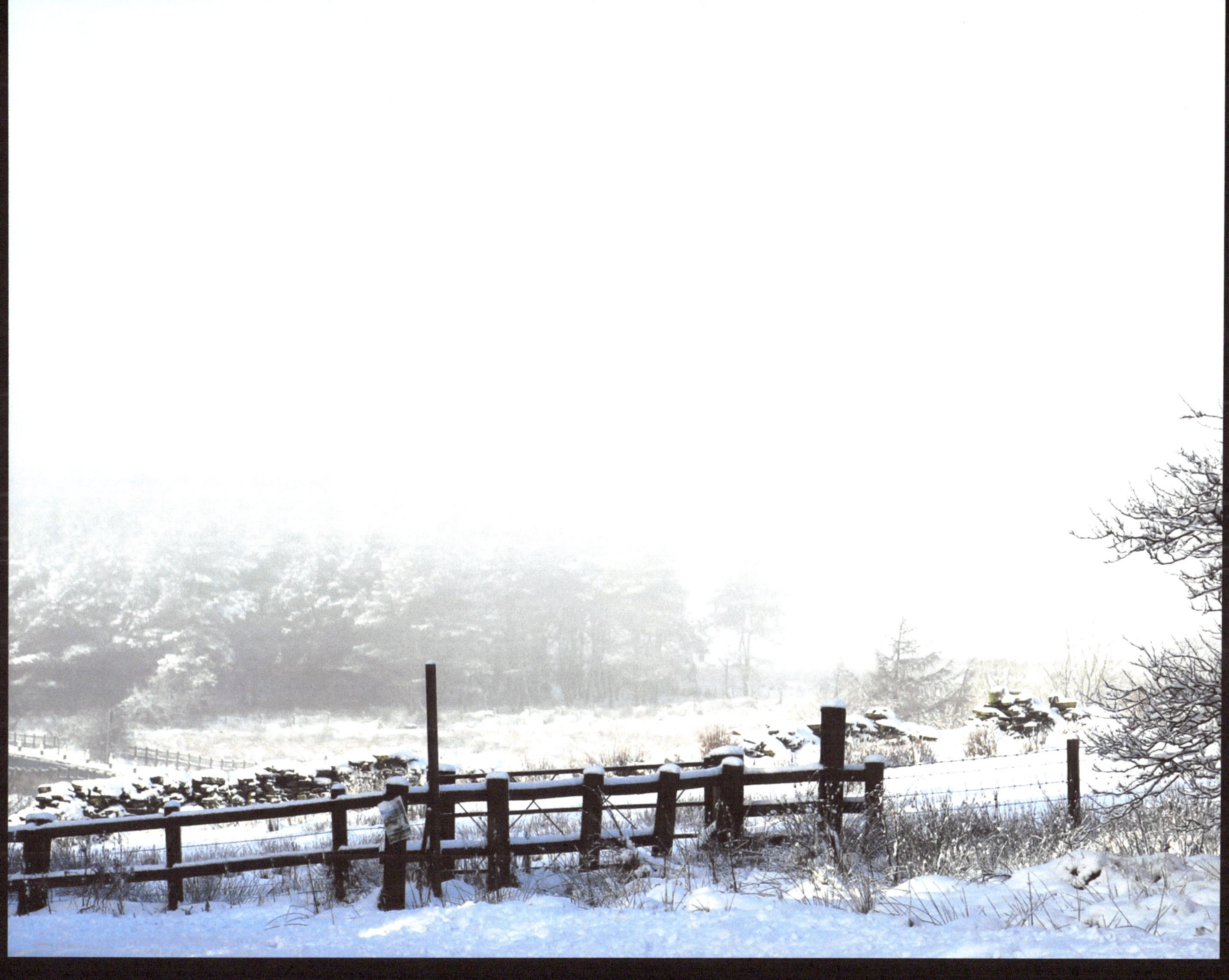

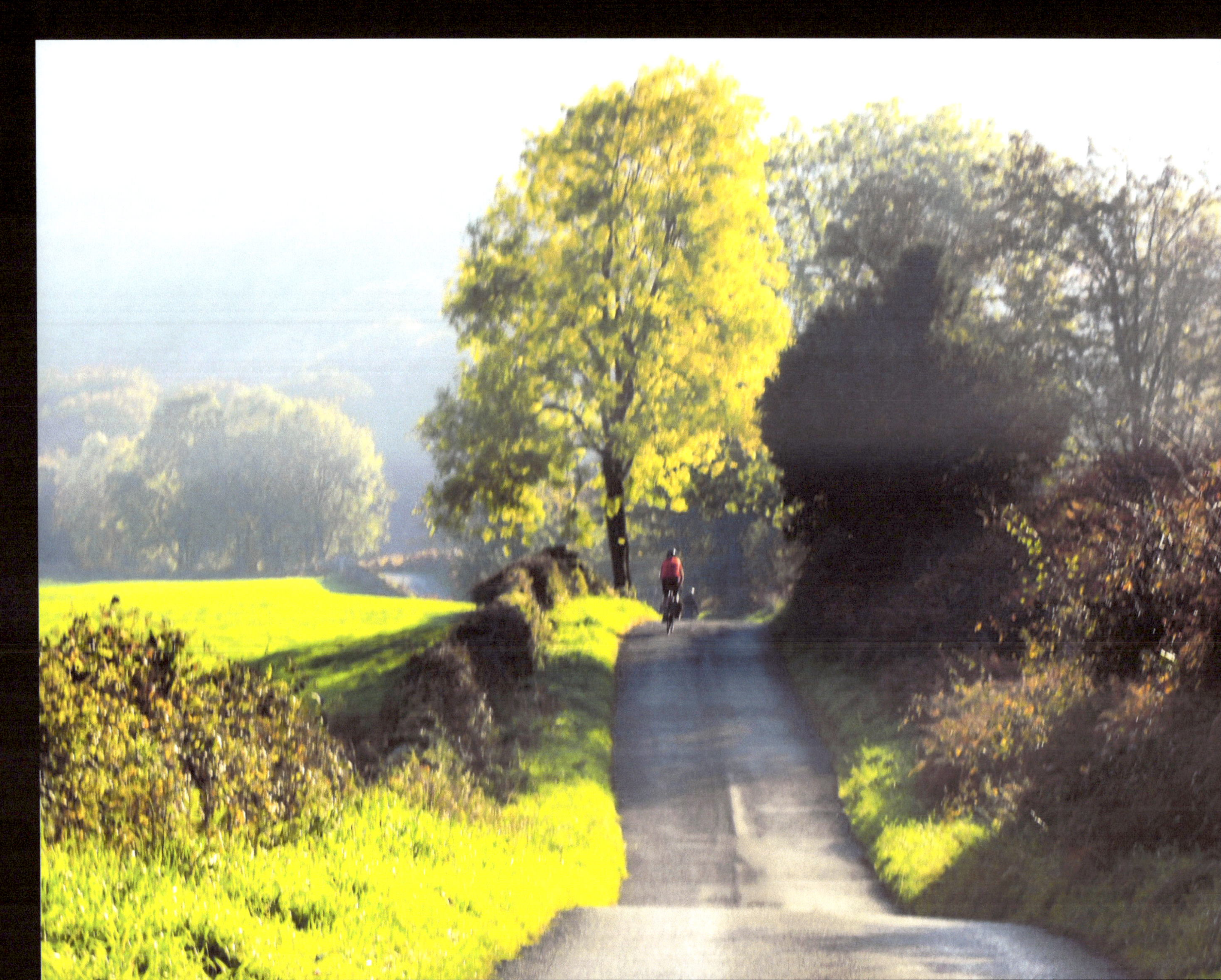

What is this sense of dullness, this dis-ease
Which weighs upon the spirit and disrupts
the mind?
Which neither food nor drink nor friendship
can allay.
For though we sip of this and taste of that,
We find no respite, no comfort for the heart.
And then, it seems by chance,
In Truth with greatest care,
A veil shifts aside
To leave revealed a fullness,
A sweetness which does not cloy.....
And joy.
And where now the lack, the sense of staleness?
Was it ever really there
Or did we dream it?

And O the world seemed so full of joy on that warm spring morning as I watched the children running across the meadow, their skirts flowing, their hair flying, each strand lustrous, shining like silk. And did their feet really touch the ground, or did they dance on air and lightly skim the surface like swallows on a lake? I know not, but ah, I thought them goddesses in their infinite beauty and grace, as they played in a land all gleaming green and golden.

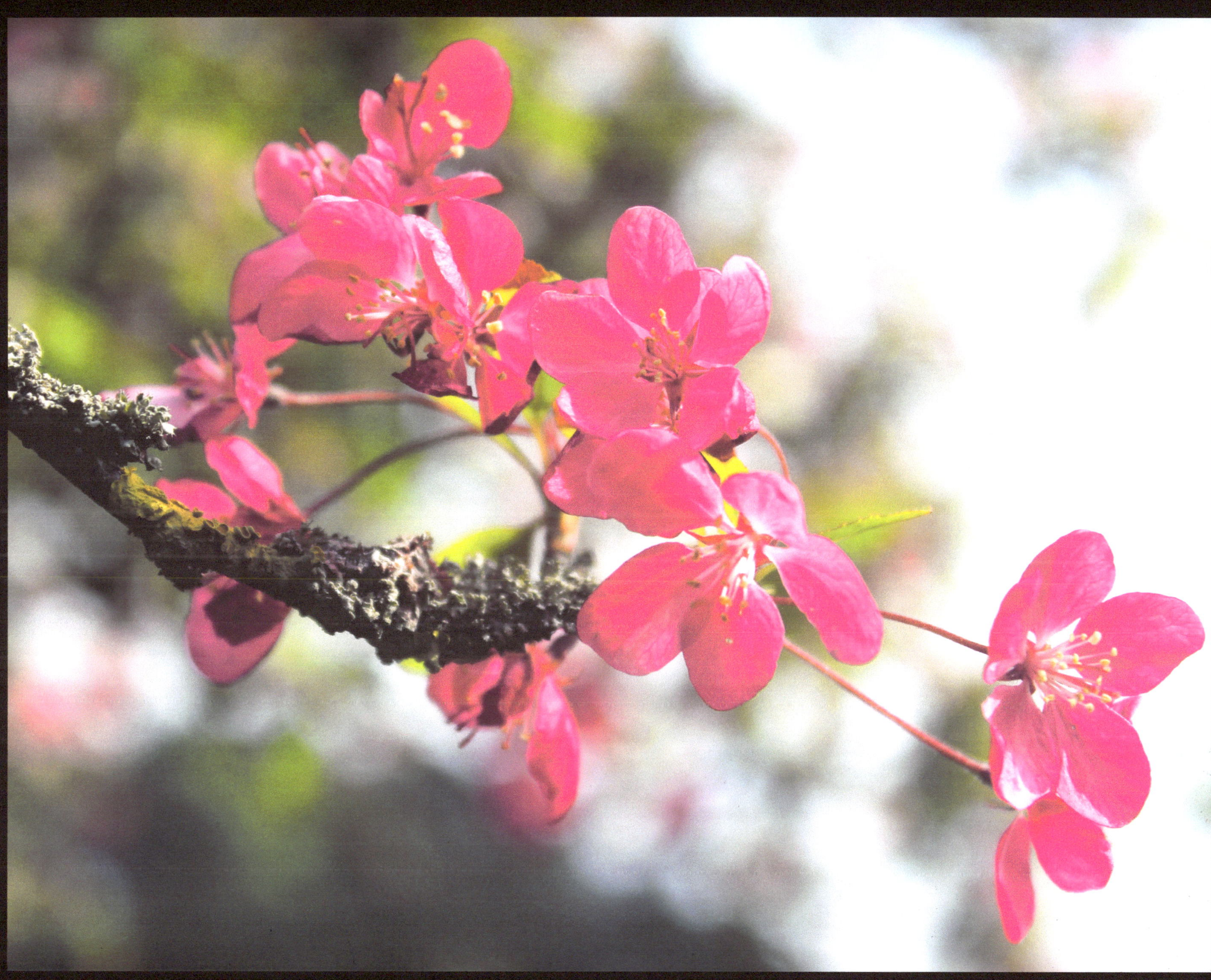

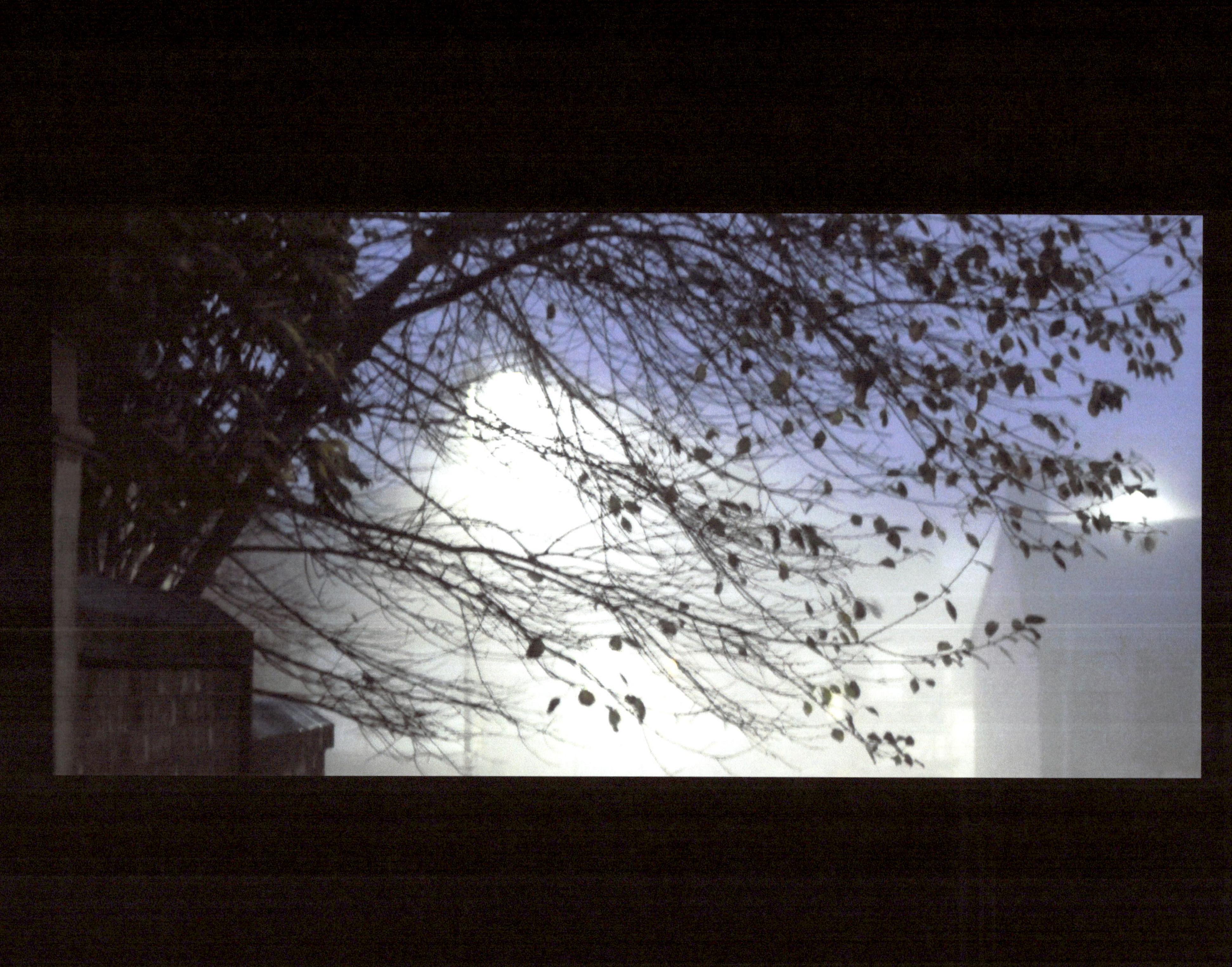

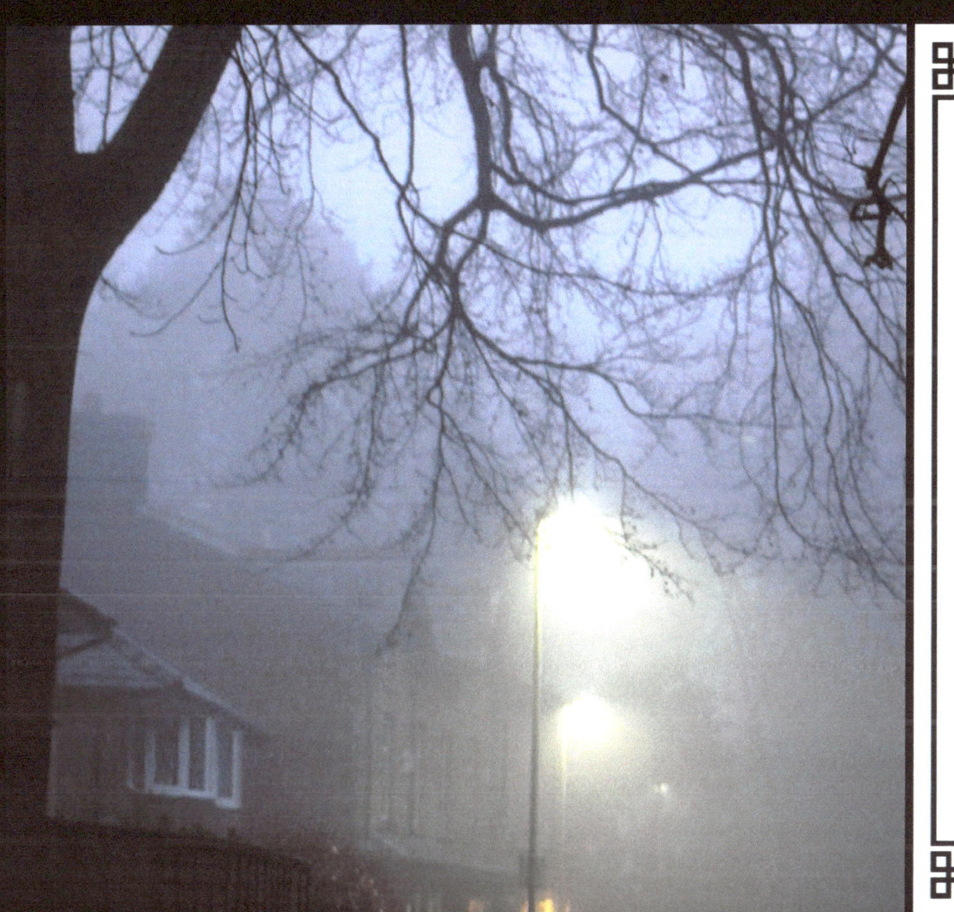

From the brow of the hill we could see lights dimly gleaming in the dusky autumn evening. We drove down the hill, through the quiet village and up the road which winds its way through the woods. We felt a sense of coming home, of returning to a place familiar and deeply loved.

The world is charged with the grandeur of God.
It will flame out, like shining from shook foil;
It gathers to a greatness, like the ooze of oil
Crushed. Why do men then now not reck his rod?
Generations have trod, have trod, have trod;
And all is seared with trade; bleared, smeared
with toil;
And wears man's smudge and shares man's smell:
the soil
Is bare now, nor can foot feel, being shod.

And for all this, nature is never spent;
There lives the dearest freshness deep down things;
And though the last lights off the black
West went
Oh, morning, at the brown brink
eastward, springs –
Because the Holy Ghost over the bent
World broods with warm breast
and with ah! bright wings.

Gerard Manley Hopkins (1844–1899)

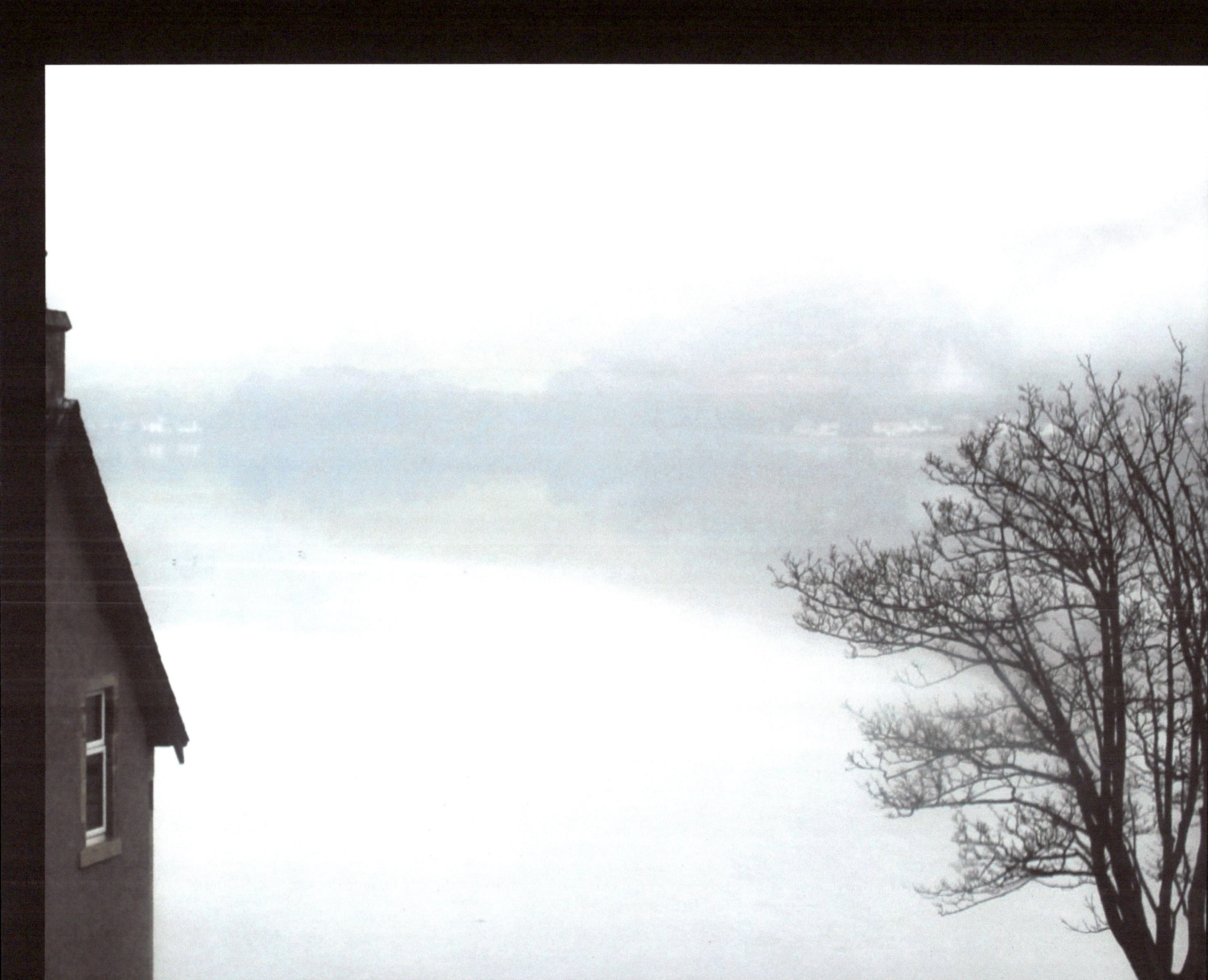

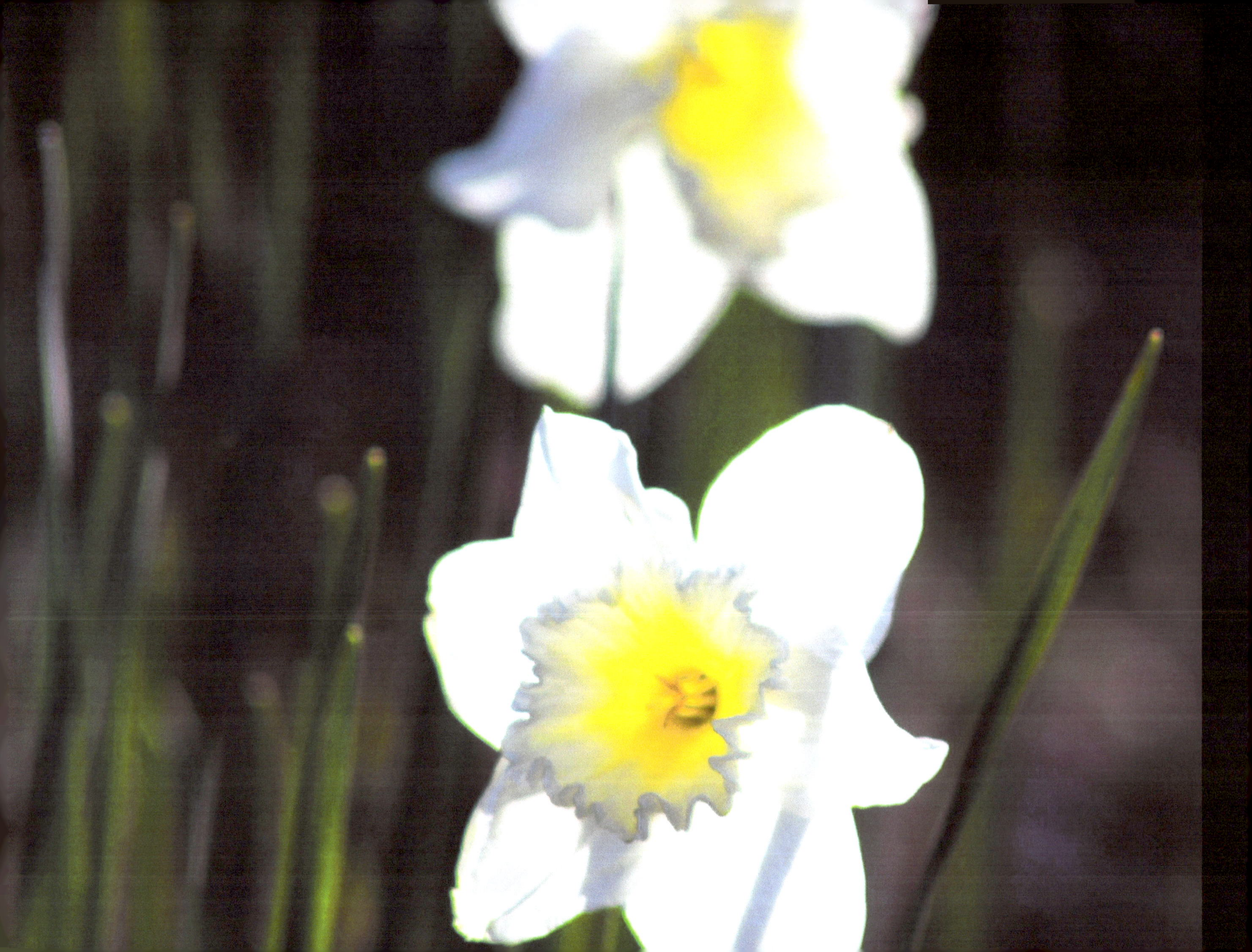

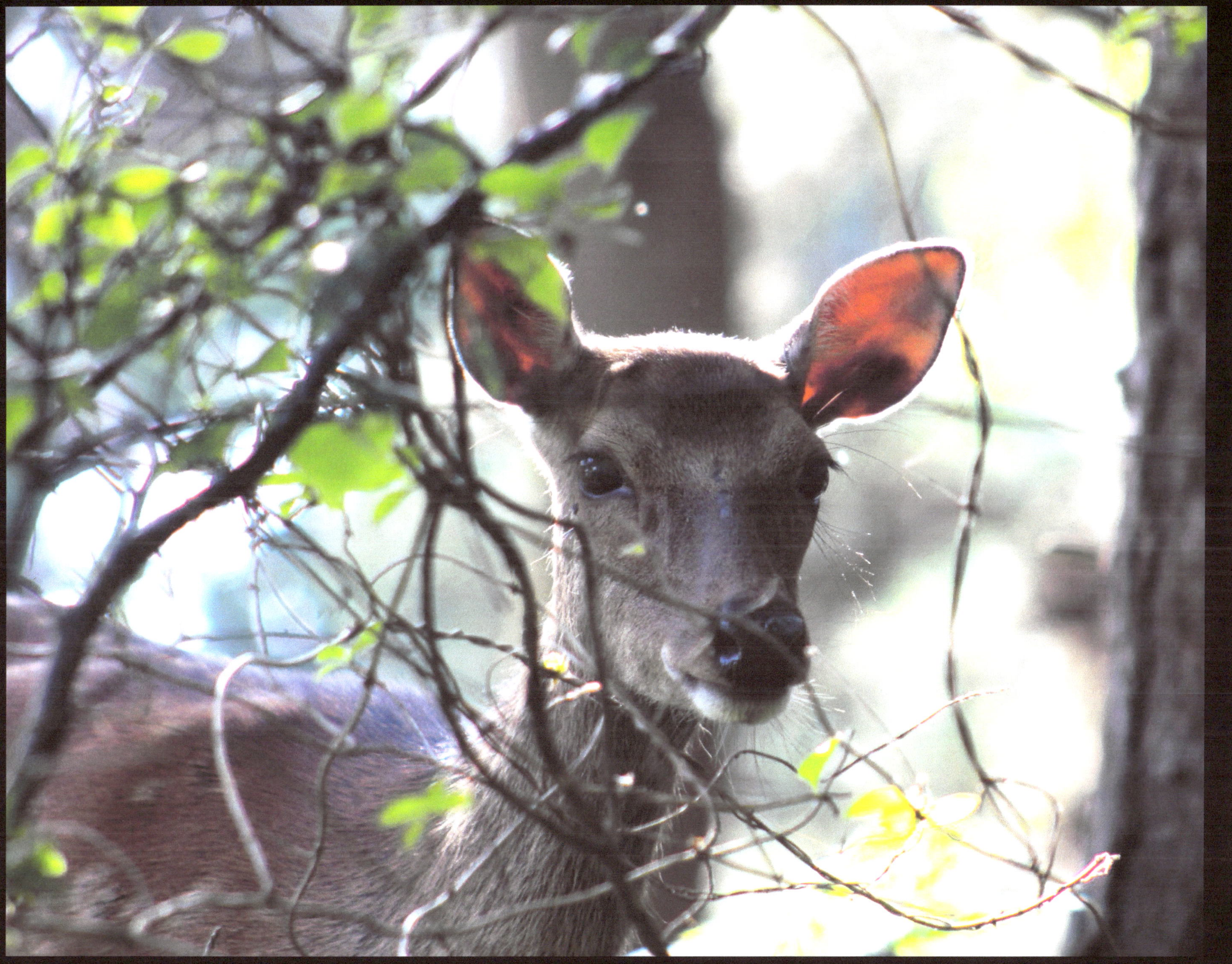

We walk through a world enclosed in mist, and the light is pearly and opaque, faintly luminous and as softly beautiful as mother-of-pearl. A tall pine lifts great branches to the sky as if in praise, and horses move in their paddocks, their coats moist and gleaming. Each tree or hedge, each gate, every blade of grass, appears and stands revealed in such awesome, such utter beauty, that even to speak would seem a desecration.

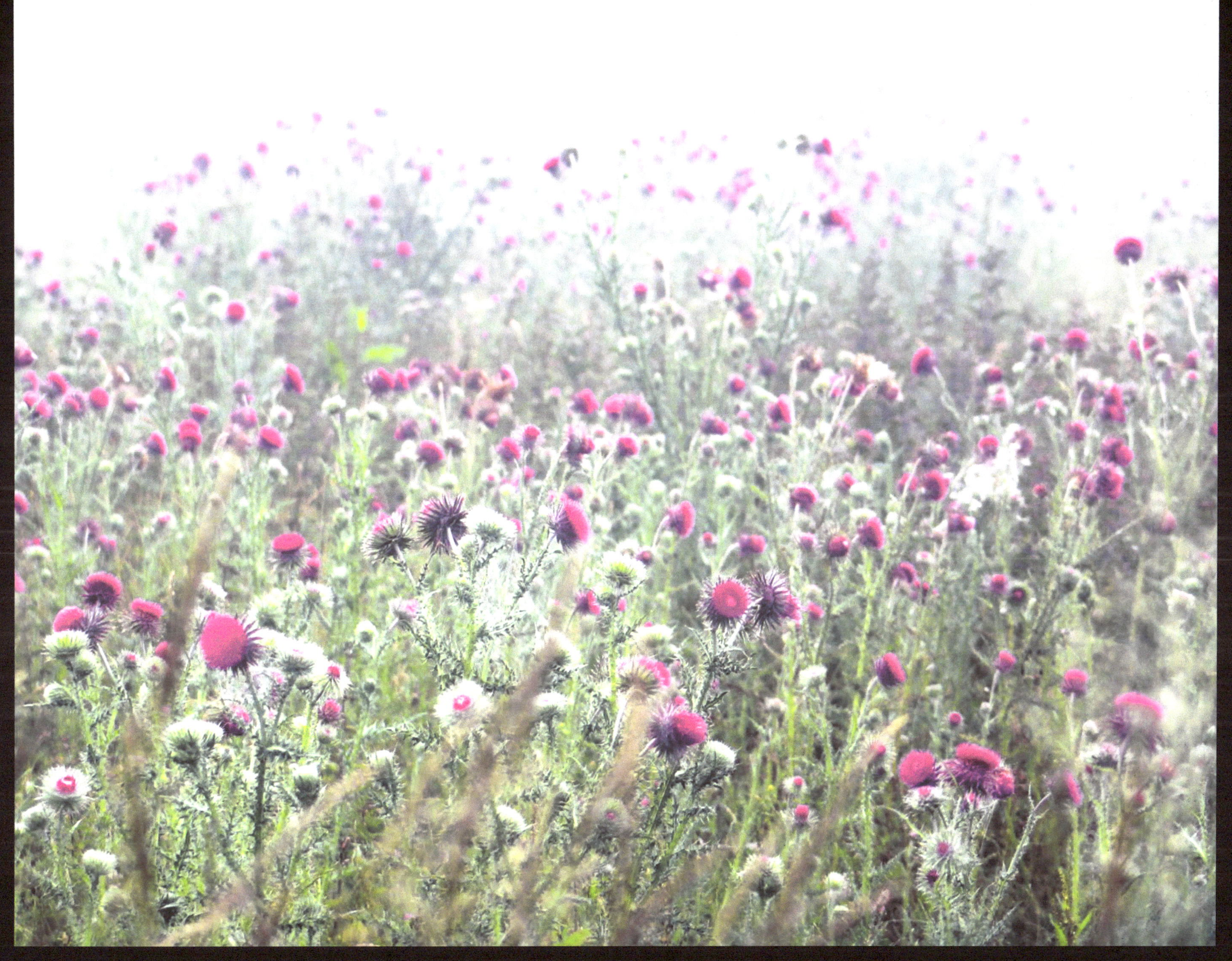

The church bells began to ring as I left the old stone bridge which spans the stream with the cottages lining its banks. As I walked along the narrow lane where the bramble and roses tumble over high walls, the peals rang out over the village; rang out over cottages glowing warm in the evening light, rang out over the stream where the swans feed beneath the willows, rang out and out over meadows and pastures, and beyond to the golden and fragrant mist of corn as it rose up to meet the sky in long sweeping curves. And the bells carried the sound of gladness, of exultation, to spread like a balm over the valley, to the blue line of the hills beyond. I looked back down the lane, to the village in its fold of hills, and in that moment the land and all its people seemed unutterably dear. The joy and love, so tangible, so abundant and full, I knew to be universal and eternal and by nature divine, and felt myself to be the most blessed of men.

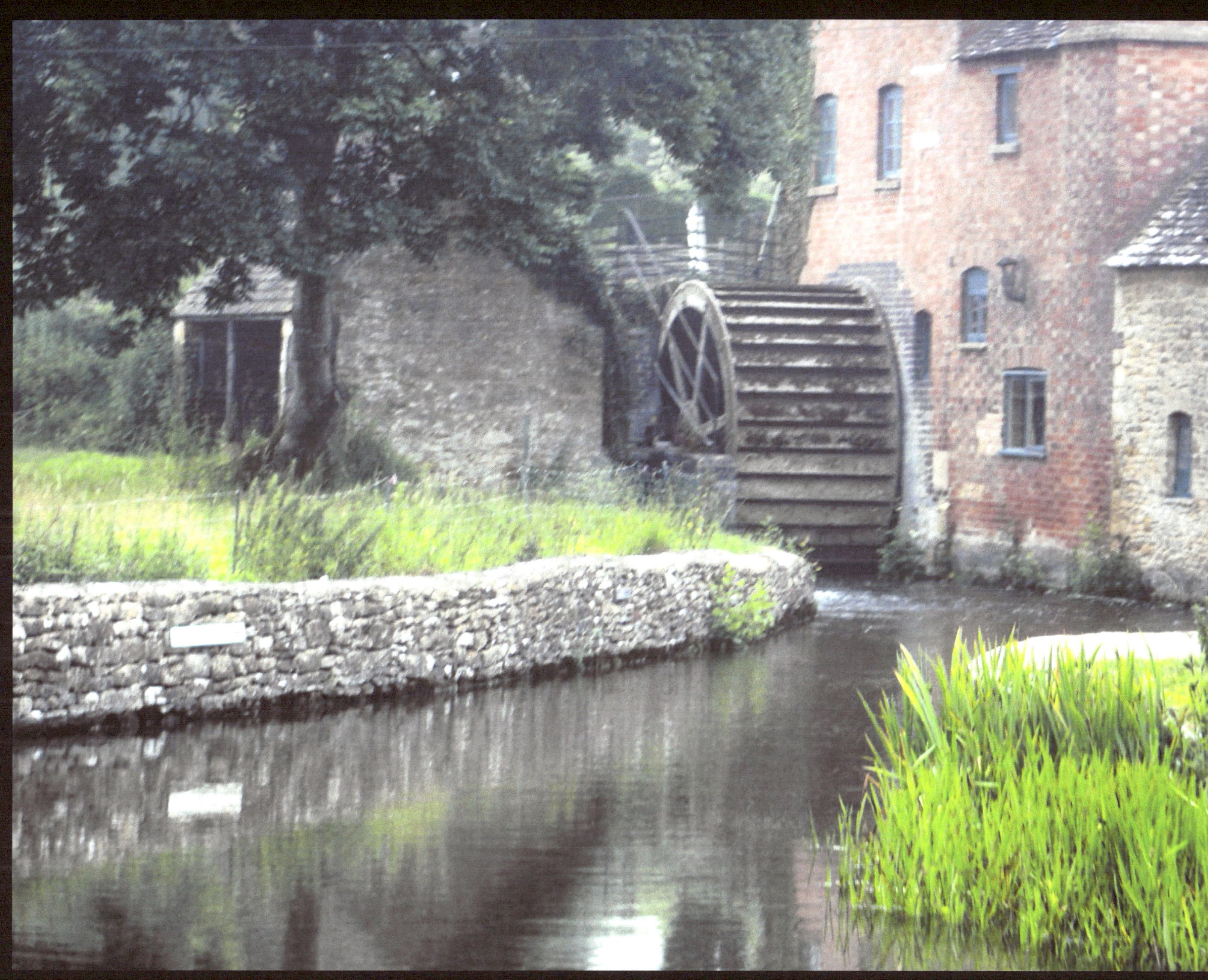

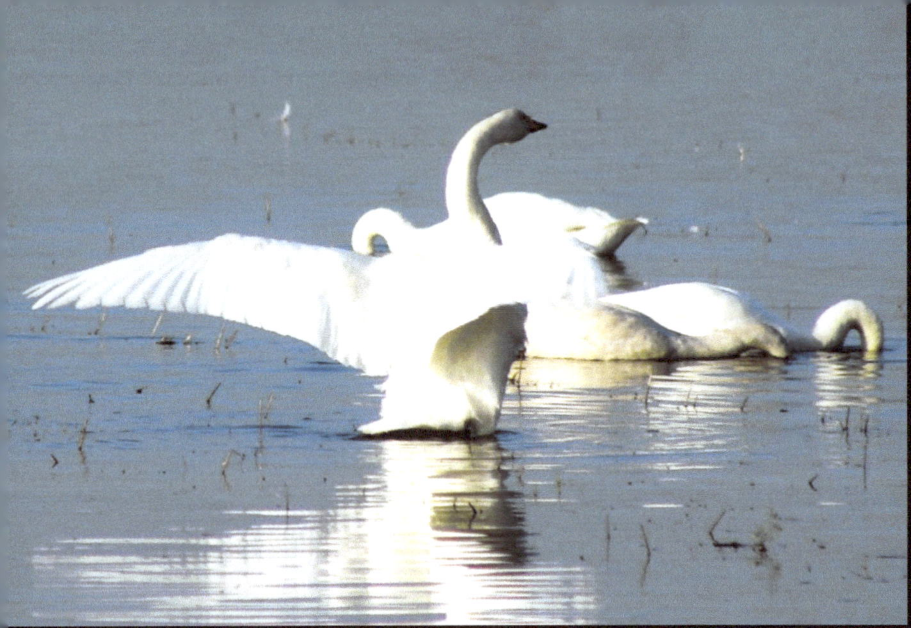

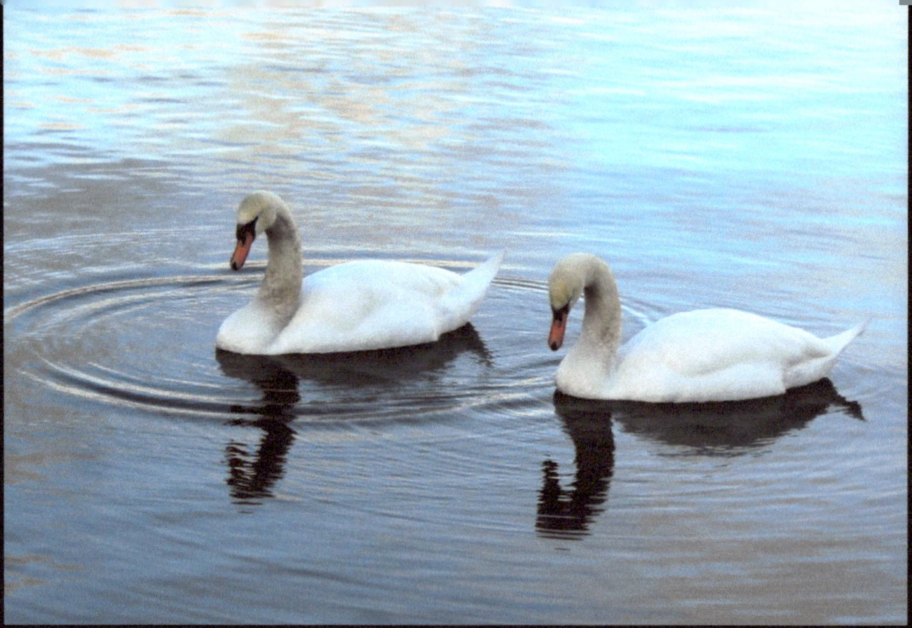

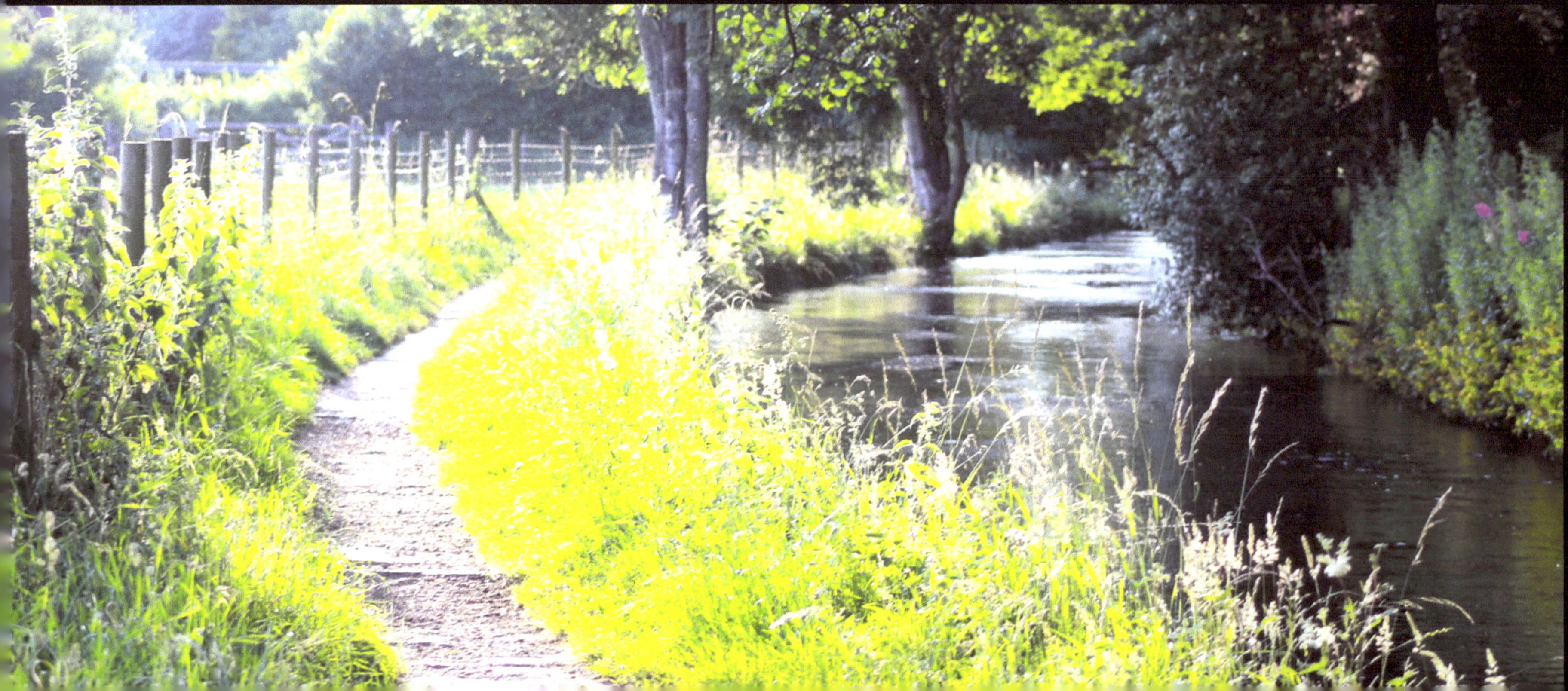

Here the banks rose steeply on either side of the road, with trees forming a living wall of richest colour; a living tapestry towering up and up into the sunlit haze; a tapestry aflame with autumn's greens, reds and golds, stretching for mile upon mile, then opening into a broad valley, to lie spread over fields, beside rivers, covering vast acres, covering realms, spreading out before the eyes in glory and majesty.

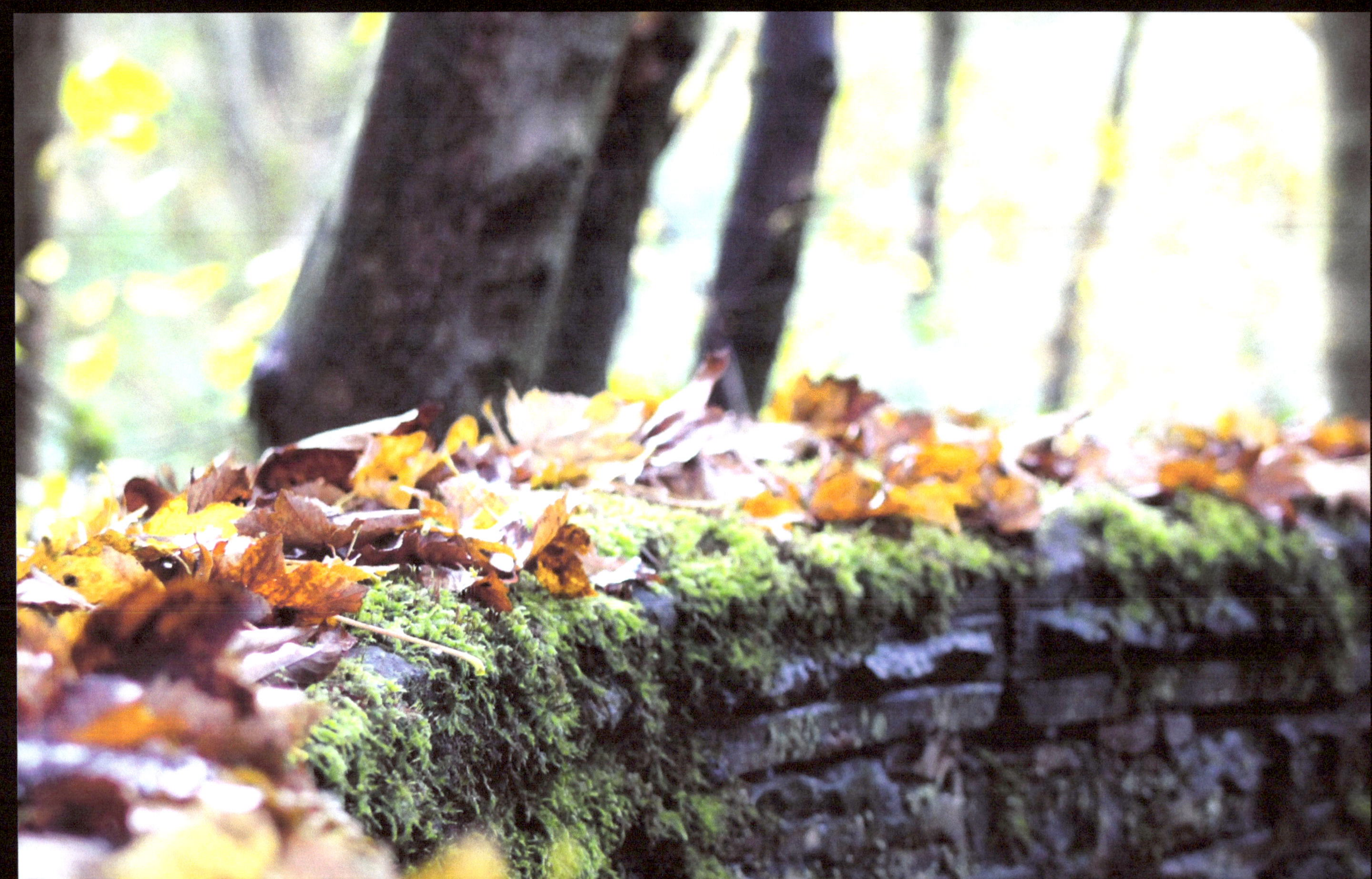

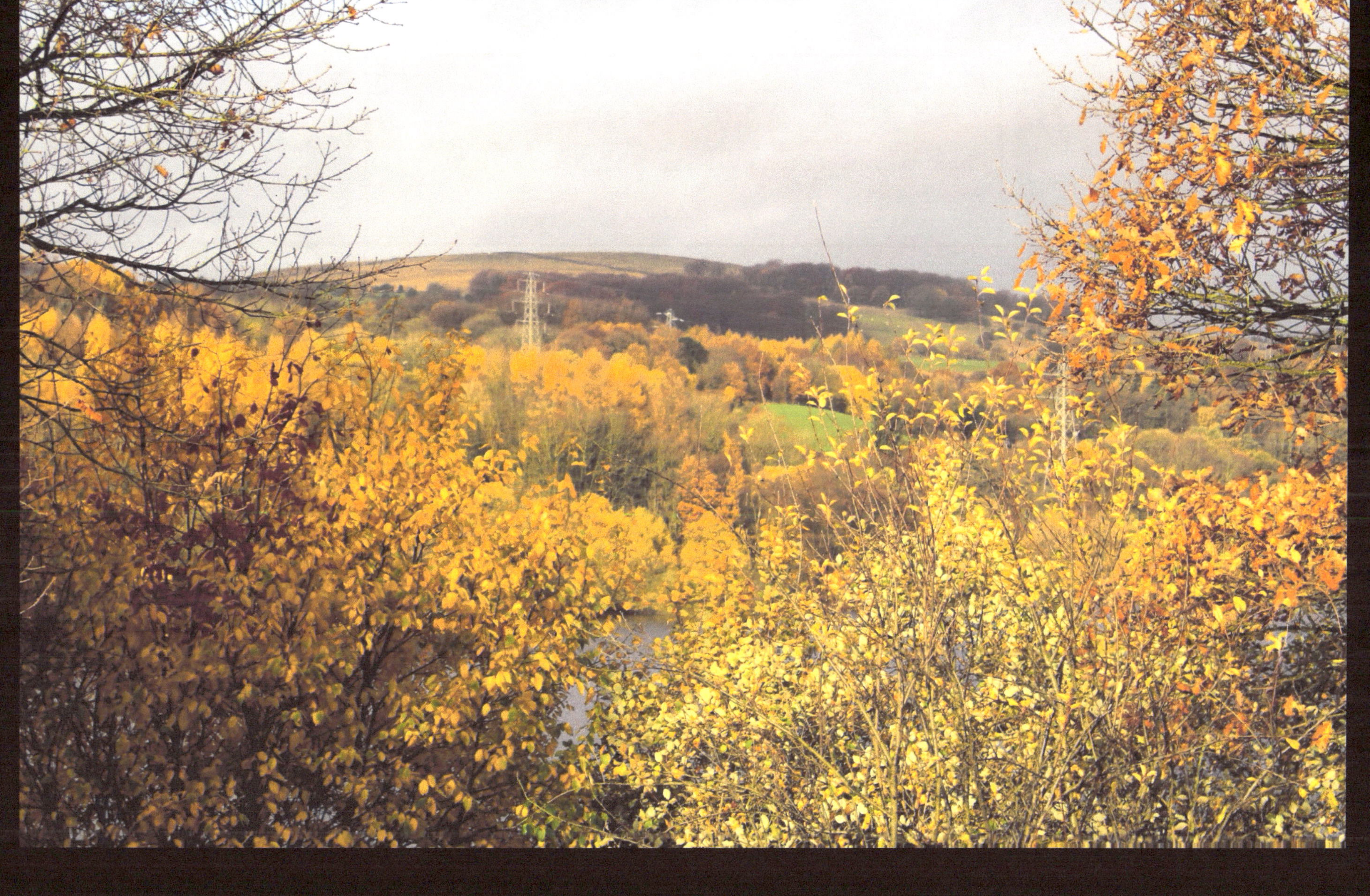

I am given a gift; an apple, brilliant red like precious glass, cool and smooth in my hand, and I sense the rougher texture of the flesh beneath the thin skin. Holding it to the light from the window, I see reflected the window panes, the trees and sky and a single snowdrop growing on the window-ledge. It seems that the whole world, indeed, even the universe, is reflected there; the rivers and oceans, the continents, stars, planets and galaxies, all there, as one, held in the palm of my hand.

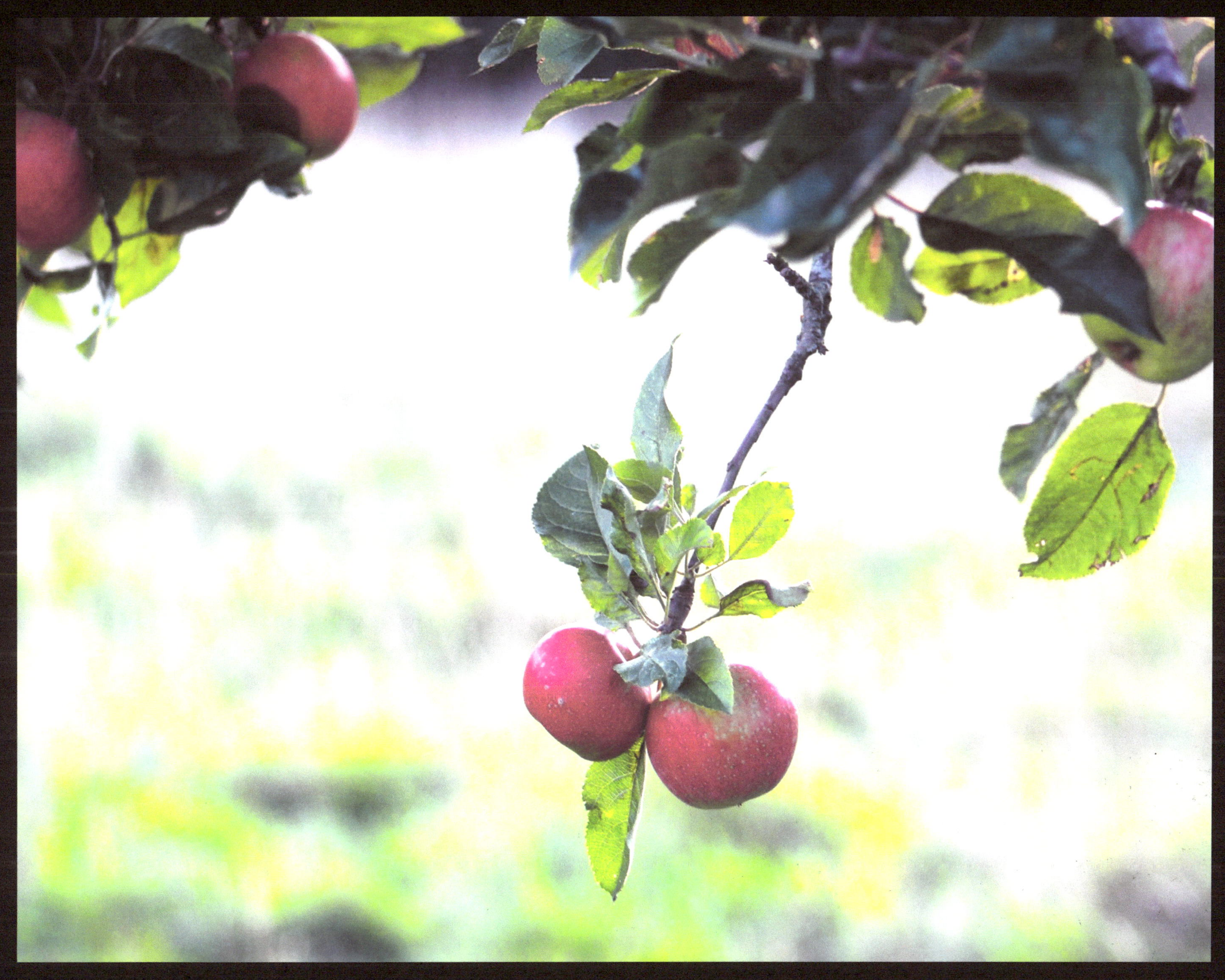

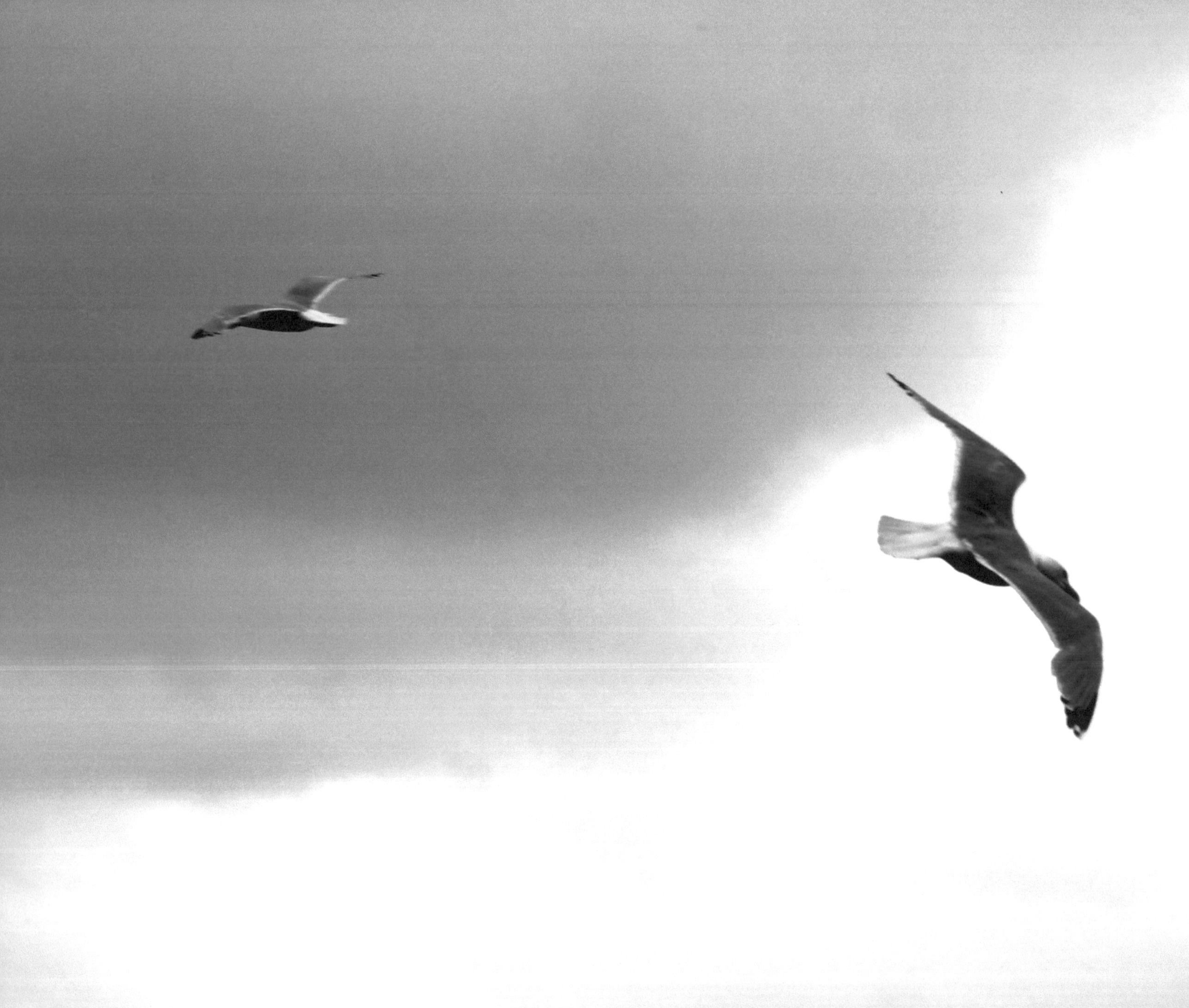

And After The Rain, The Light Comes Flooding Over Fields Veiled In Mist. A Flock Of Birds, Brilliant White, Ethereal, Circles And Soars, Held In A Shaft Of Silver, Caught There And Held In The Immortal Moment.

In gathering dusk, the meadows beyond the hedges appeared shadowy, their borders blurred and indistinct, veiled in mist. Lights from the cottages gleamed dimly across the green, and a welcoming shaft of light spilled from the window of the inn at the side of the road. Beams of light from a passing car appeared above a rise in the lane, bathing trees and hedgerows in a sudden splash of silver, making the gloom radiant and beautiful. Here and there, at intervals along the narrow lanes, street lamps made quiet pools of brightness in the darkness. As dusk deepened, the visible world became the dark shape of cattle in the fields, the dark, enclosing line of hedges, the dark bulk of distant woods in a sea of grey. Under cottage roofs, in the glow of lamplight, family life turned inwards, thoughts turned to homely things; the home appeared as a haven of security and peace. And darkness fell and settled on the land.

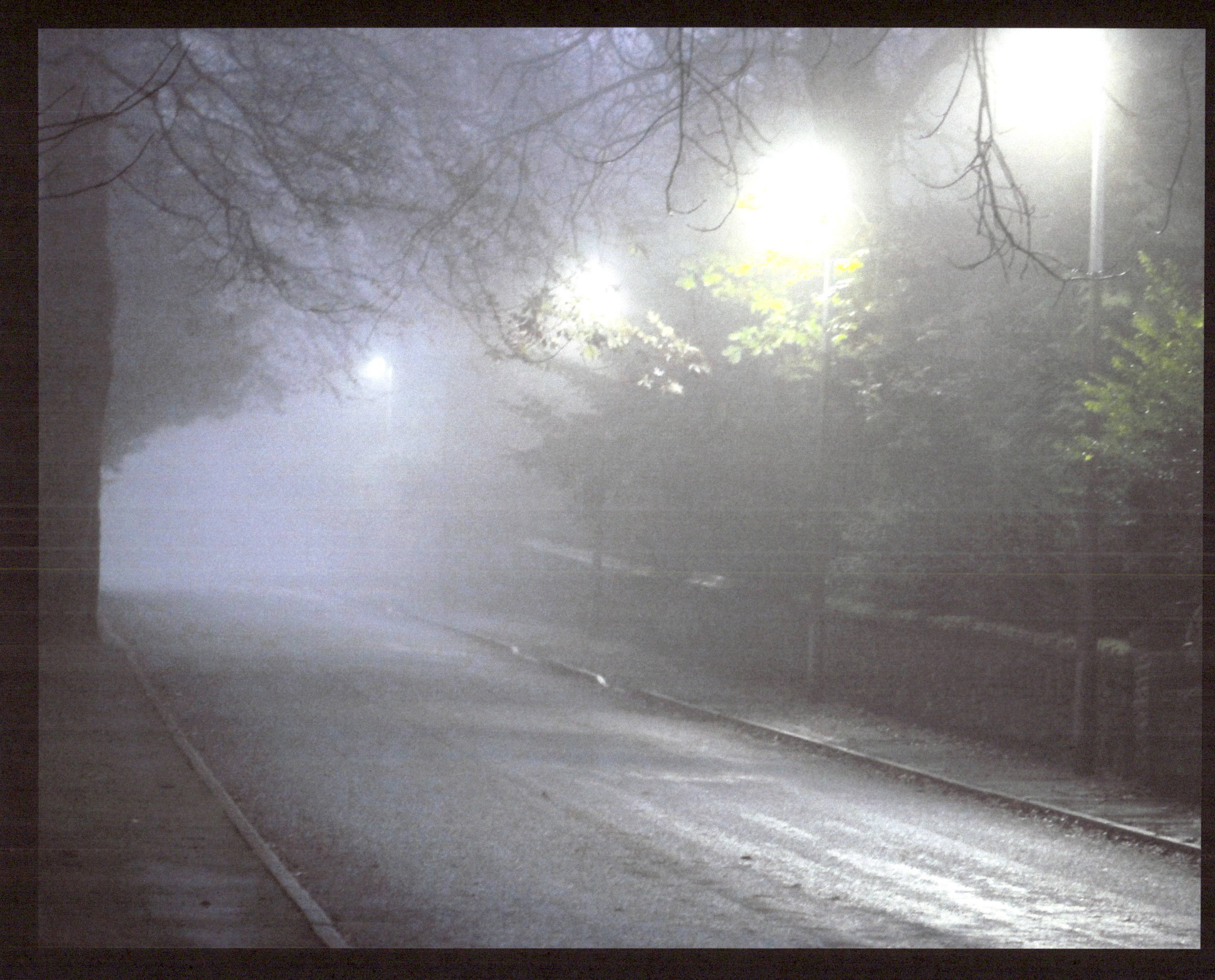

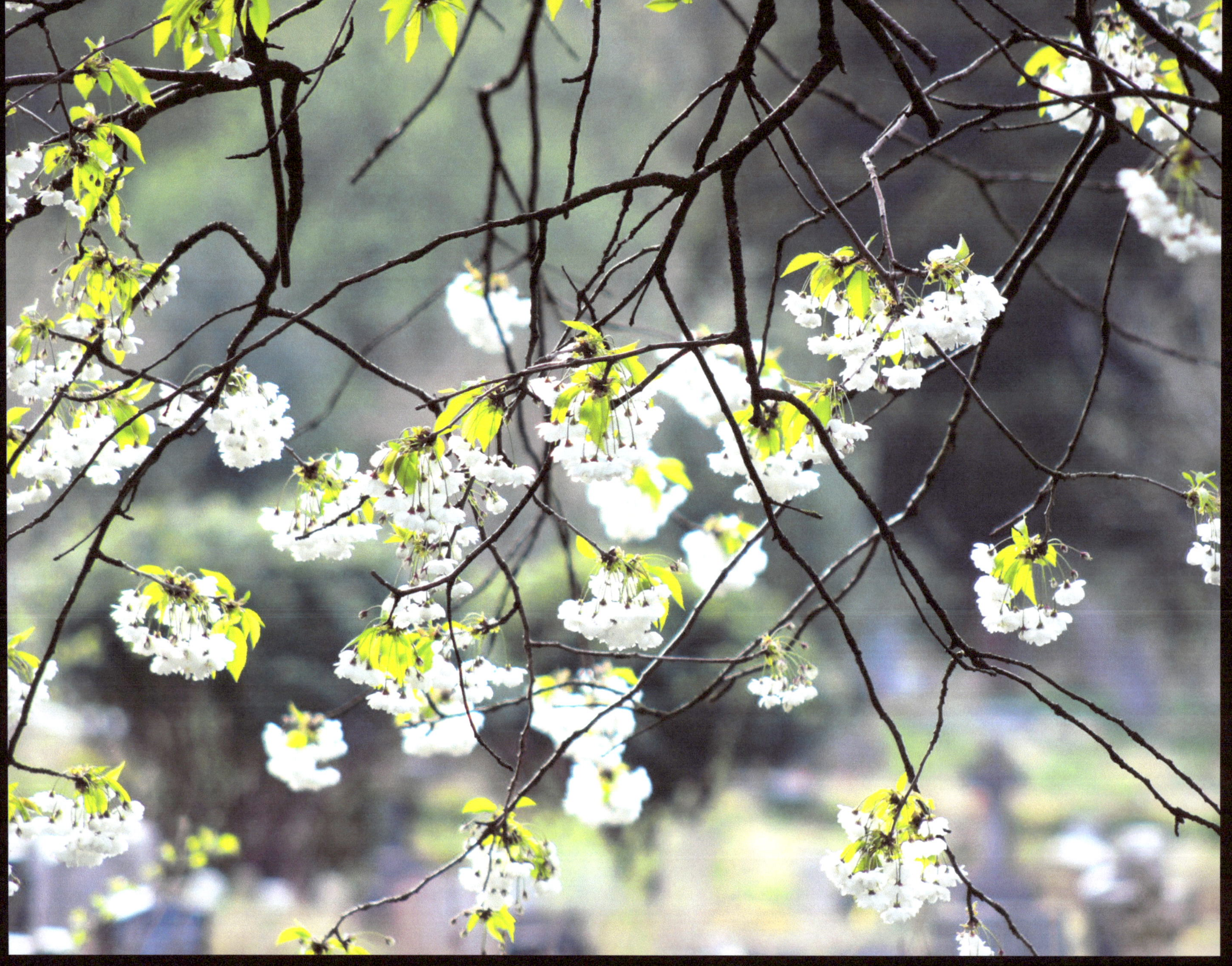

Around the war graves the people stand in appreciation of those who gave their lives that we might know goodness and freedom in ours.

The mood is sombre, tinged with sadness as they stand.

Now the trumpeter, waiting on the lawns amidst the bluebells and dandelion, lifts his trumpet to his lips and the piercingly sad notes of The Last Post, drift down over the crowd, down the valley, and up and up into the blossoms and the treetops.

An old soldier stands proud in his uniform and medals, eyes glinting with tears of loss. So sad, so regretful...

But listen, just listen! Because all the while the blackbird sings the everlasting joy.

My eyes see autumnal trees ablaze in morning's light, and shadows touching dew-fresh lawns, sprinkled with fallen leaves and scattered dandelion. They see the glinting jewels of moisture set in the springy turf, the bright light and the deep shade. But the heart knows no such thing, because it senses golden shafts of radiance pouring forth from a point of stillness, to disperse and scatter as droplets of water, in an act of creation.

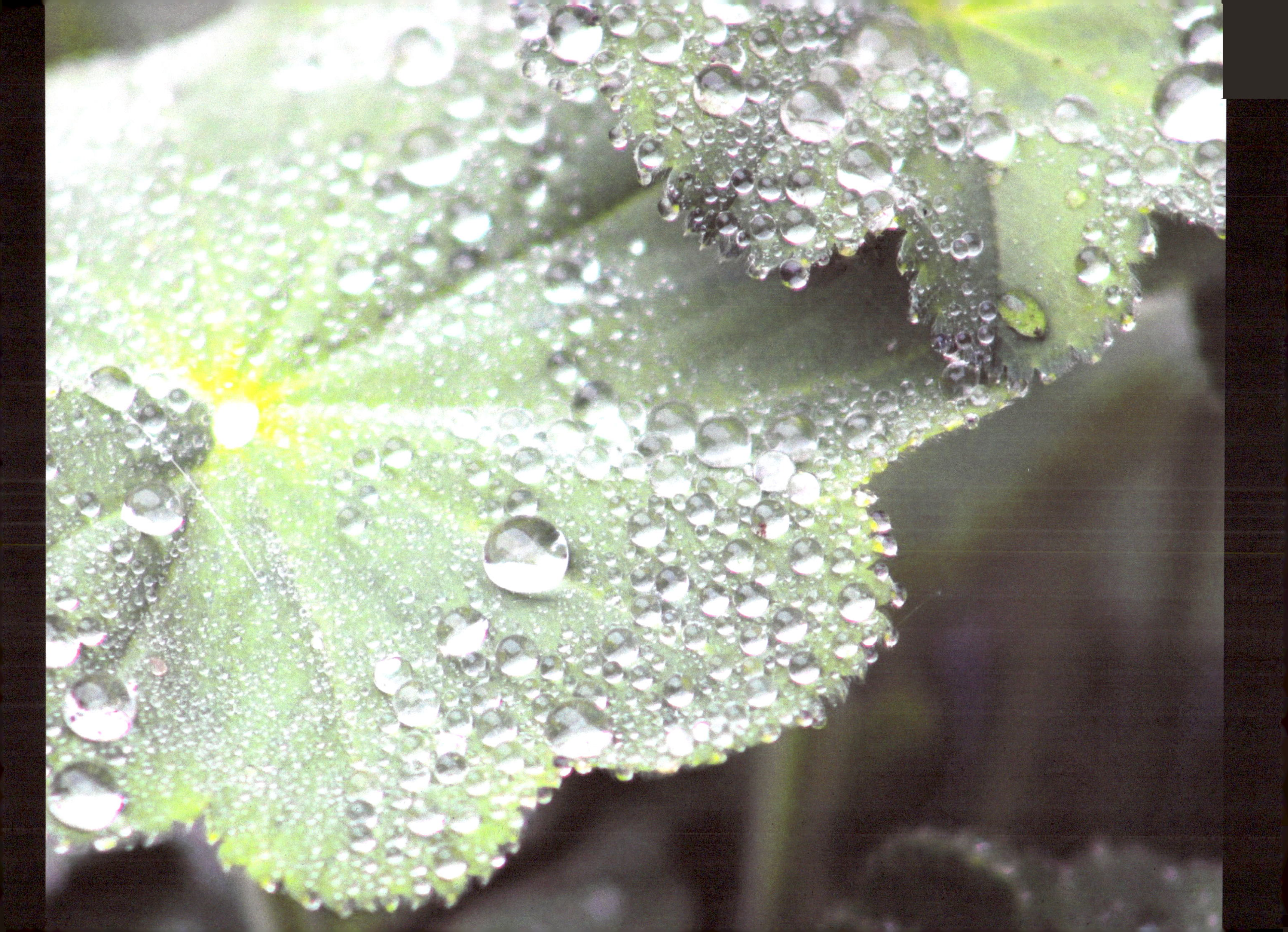

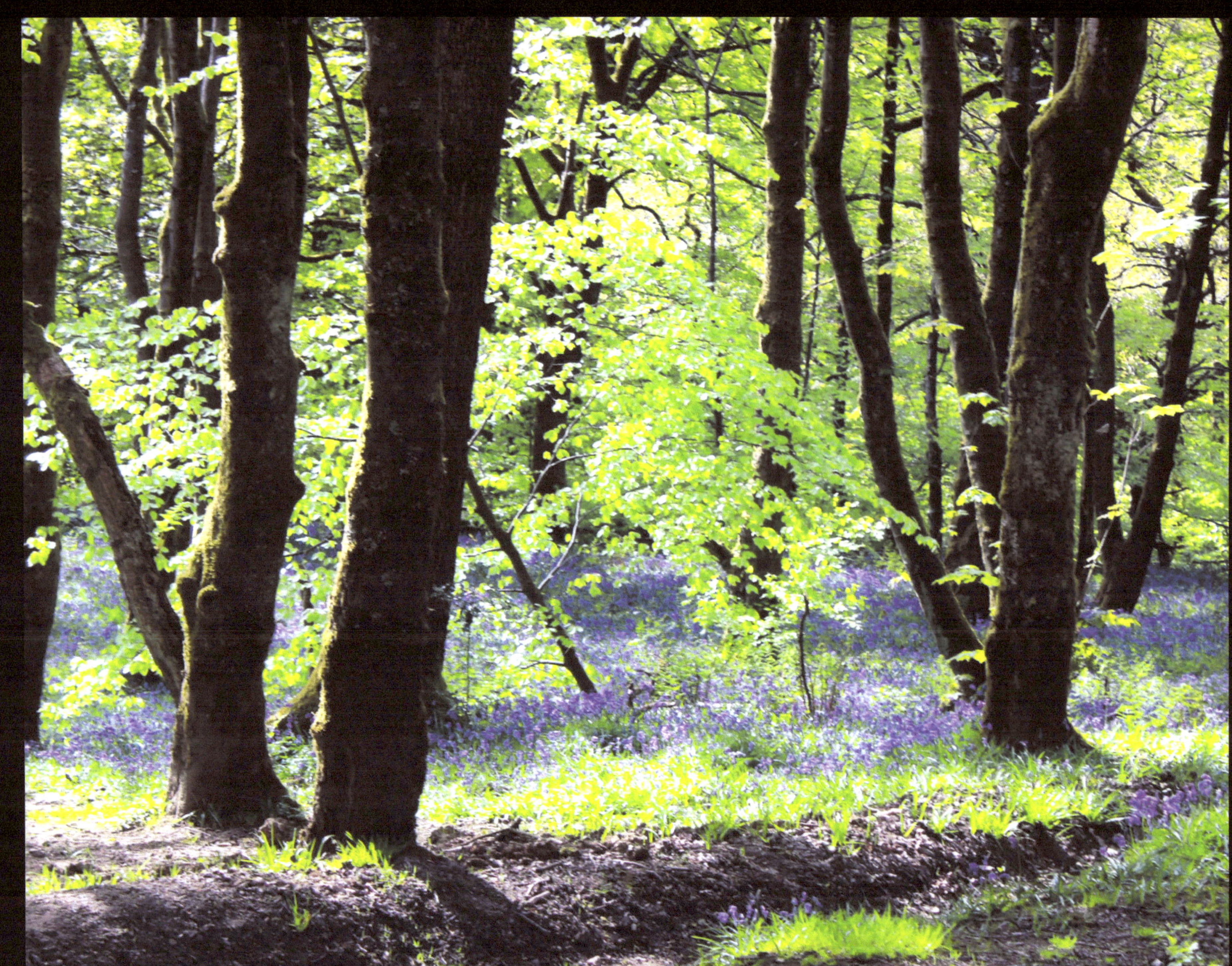

Deep in the darkness of a winter's day,
When icy frost makes white the wind-swept land,
Weary, I sometimes wish the world away.
Alone I stand;
Then quiet,
Remember Thee,
Remember joy.
And in rememb'ring find,
Meadows gold with daffodil,
And woodland floor a drift of blue.
All tender leaf,
All silv'ry light,
And air made sweet with song of bird.
All summer's green,
All summer's warmth,
And winter fled away.

Written after seeing bluebells in the wood
in Amersham, Buckinghamshire.

It is a time of mists, of cool, crisp mornings, exhilarating in their freshness. A time when leaves, bright as gemstones, clothe the branches of lofty trees.

Soon they will begin to fall, to drift down through the air like golden rain.

In the orchard, boughs heavy with ripened fruit and wet with fresh-fallen rain, cascade over the old stone walls.

Faded roses still adorn the churchyard wall and down in the meadow, near the old well, ragged seedheads are all that speak of the flowers of summer and are a promise of their return in the springtime.

Now all is changing as the days shorten, as autumn moves towards the winter. Ripened berries glow warm in cottage gardens and a mantle of crimson ivy bedecks the lovely old inn on the edge of the green.

And now, in the gardens, pastures and fields, over all the land, it is a time of gratitude, of thanksgiving, a time of plenty. It is time for the harvest to be gathered in.

A time of quiet beauty, of mellow days, a time of evenings around the fire with those we love.

And all of the abundance, all of the beauty, all of the love is held in the everlasting and unchanging glory of God's love and light.

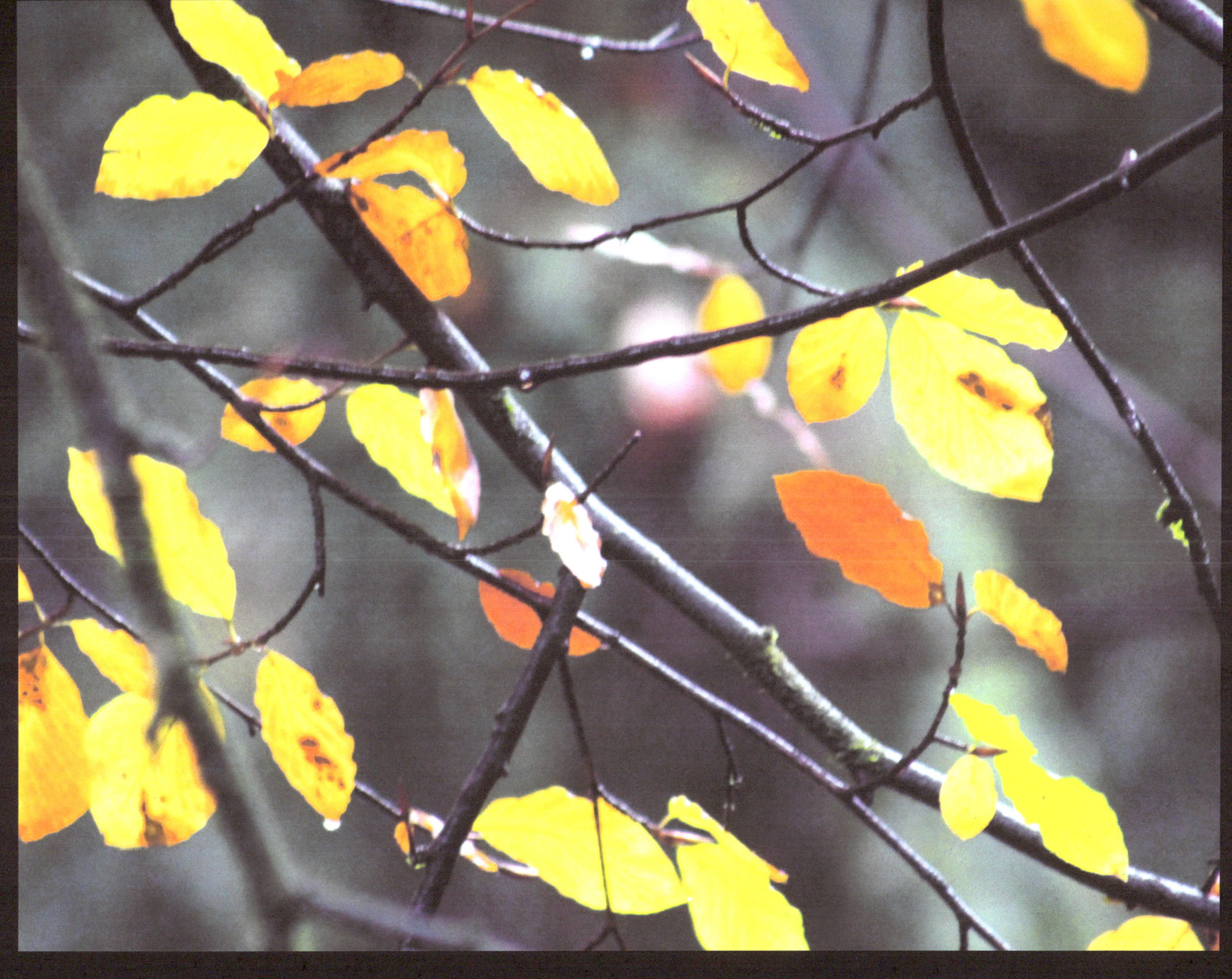

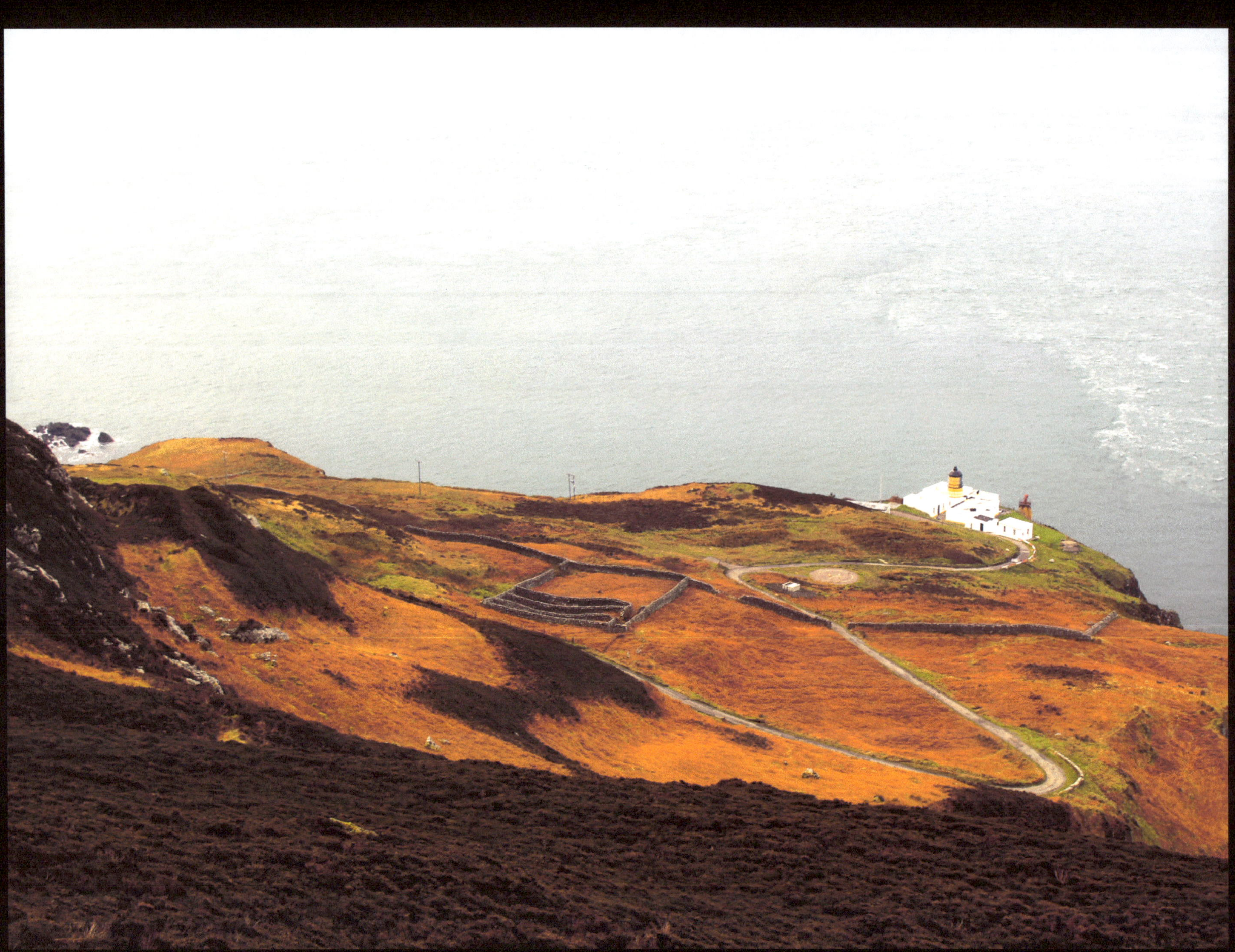

Photograph taken by Glynnis Carthy

How shall I tell of this place unless it is to speak of the winds sighing through the long grasses?

Or shall I speak of the deep peace of the high hills, the distant, sweet bleating of the lambs and the answering call of their dams?

Or perhaps of the pearly waterfall leaping and splashing over the rocks, to fall, to plunge and tumble into the deep, cool, fern-fringed pond?

Or of the cottages on its banks, sleeping against the sun-warmed crags?

Or perhaps I'll tell of the waves, far, far below, lapping rhythmically on the rocks at the foot of the lighthouse?

Or of the effortless grace of the gulls soaring and gliding above the waters, their strange, wild cries floating up and up on the pure, clear air?

Or of the fishing boat lying at anchor on a vast, vast and silent sea?

All of these things? And yet... and yet...

For the place is imbued, is suffused with an ethereal and mystical air which brings to mind those beautiful words,

"Put off thy shoes from off thy feet, for the place whereon thou standest is hallowed ground."

Mull of Kintyre, March, 2019

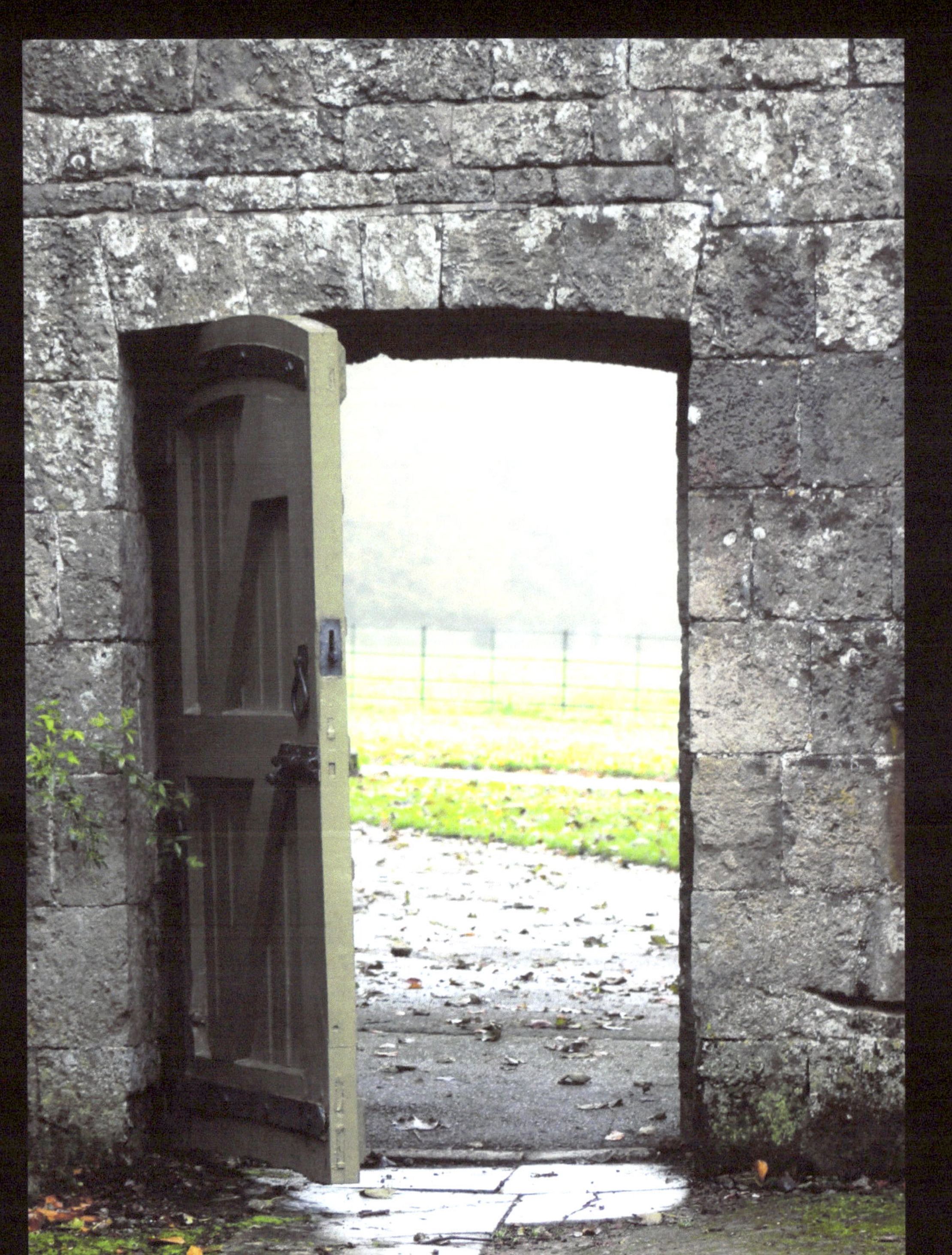

Beauty is all about us...

Goodness is all about us...

Joy is all about us...

Love is all about us...

God is all about us...

When we step over the threshold and open

Our hearts to Truth.

Written in Darwen, Lancashire.

September, 2019.

I stand and gaze as day's first light sends shafts of gold o'er misted fields,
And sound is muted, distant, low, and dawn her treasure shields.
        Then fine and clear and shining bright,
        Angelic voices floating light,
    Fill earth and sky and milky way,
    And sea and hill and windswept bay.
I stand and gaze in dawn's soft light, in golden rays on wint'ry fields,
Serene and still, at peace I stand, when heaven her secret yields.

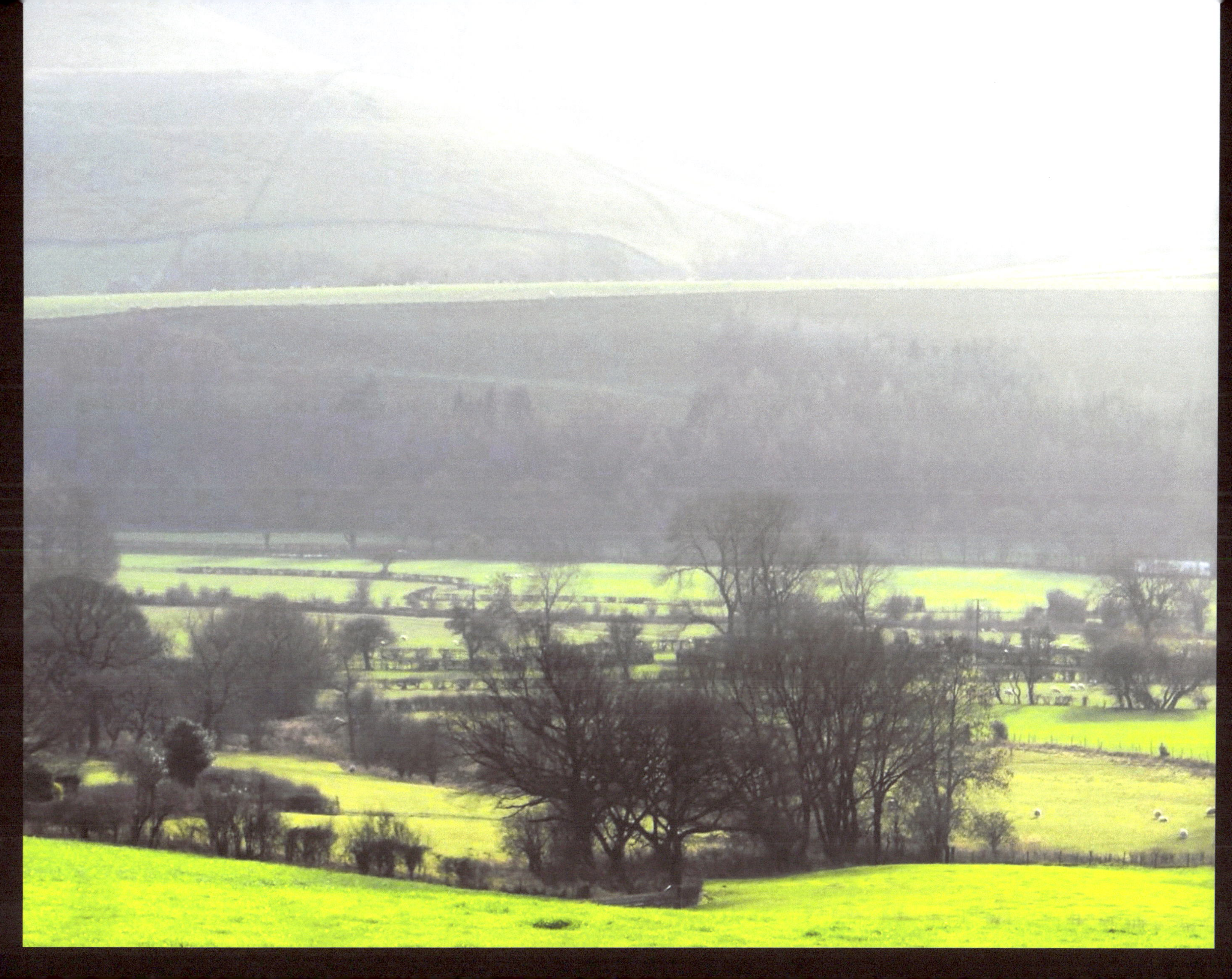

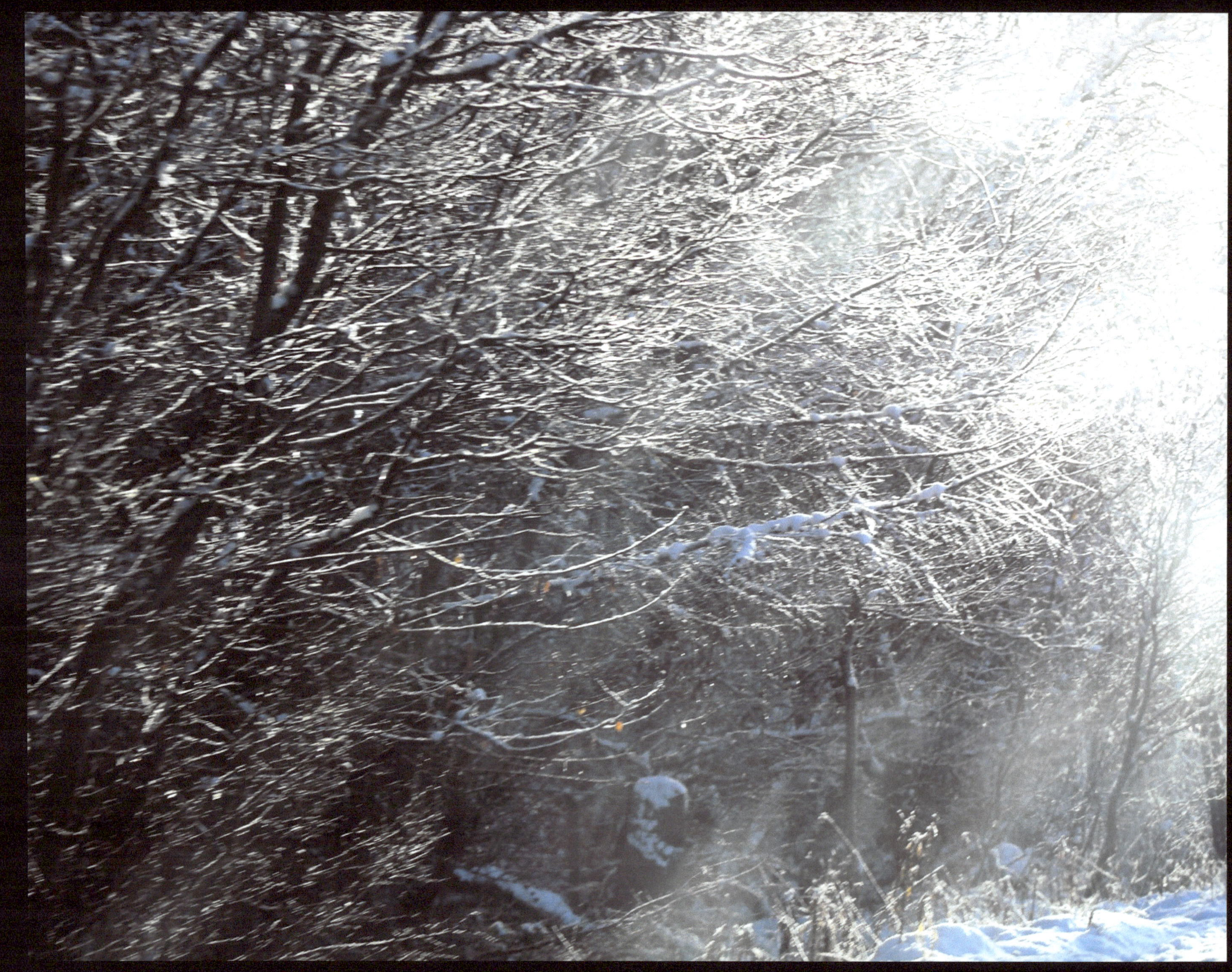

From the chair in my darkened room, I watch the snowflakes swirling and dancing in the light of a street lamp. Like showers of silvery-white gems they fall, faster now, swiftly covering the rooftops and window ledges.

As I quietly gaze, it seems that there is a shift to another realm.

Windows and walls seem to fall away. Millions and millions of snowflakes, billowing on the air, and moving faster and faster appear as stars moving across the night sky. Snow and stars and all of the great creation, merge, become one, and I am engulfed in great flurries of snow and stars, of fire and ice, all whirling, dancing, circling and driving towards and around the place where I am seated.

But I, I am untouched and unafraid, held in perfect protection and peace, secure in the everlasting presence of God.

For Phyllis. January, 2021.

To The Memory Of My Late Grandson, Antony James Carthy (1985–2013)

When he passed away, I chose, and do still choose to celebrate his life with these words:

ANTONY.

We thought his passing would bring only suffering and grief, but instead we have seen consideration and respect; gentleness and love; resolve, fortitude and strength. With humour, he laughed at misfortune and death, and brought joy to those who cared for him.

Such qualities are Divine in origin, and Godly, and flowed from the true Antony, from the deep inner core of Antony, and thus, in a sense, he showed us God, showed us Eternity.

We never saw him finer, never loved him more.

And now, strangely, yet truly, we can, in gratitude, say, "The Lord gave, and the Lord hath taken away; blessed be the name of the Lord." 1 Tim. 6:7.

9 May 2013.

What we had, what we were given and what we have gained, leaves no corner of our hearts where bitterness and despair may abide.

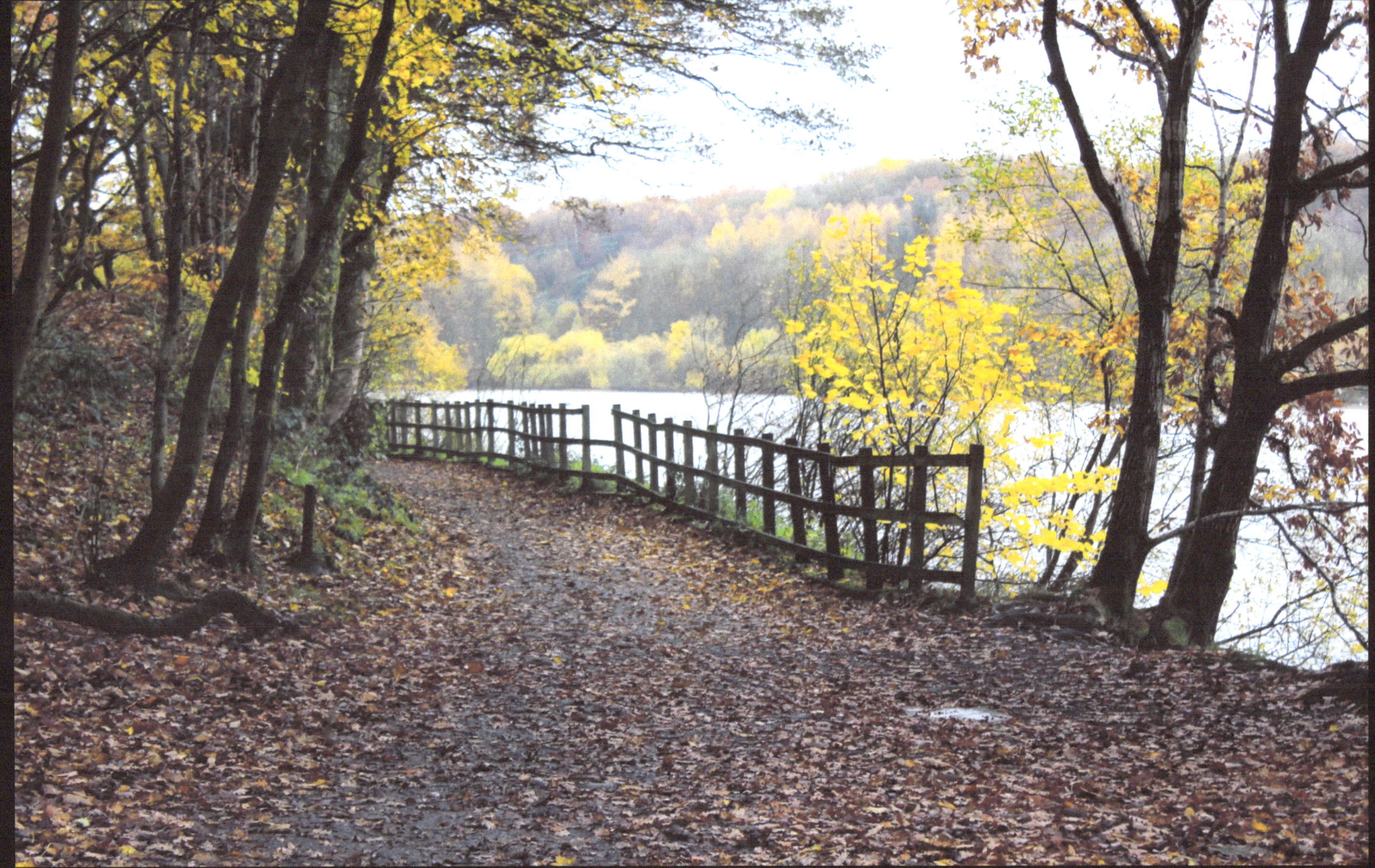

This above all: to thine own self be true,
And it must follow, as the night the day,
Thou canst not then be false to any man.

William Shakespeare

www.ingramcontent.com/pod-product-compliance
Lightning Source LLC
LaVergne TN
LVHW072329100826
845154LV00009B/146